Together in our World

RIGHTS AND EQUALITY

Marie Murray

Illustrated by Hanane Kai

free spirit
PUBLISHING®

Published in North America by Free Spirit Publishing Inc., Minneapolis, Minnesota, 2020

Library of Congress Cataloging-in-Publication Data
This book has been filed with the Library of Congress.
LCCN: 2020933297
ISBN-13: 978-1-63198-578-2

Reading Level Grade 3; Interest Level Ages 6–10
Fountas & Pinnell Guided Reading Level P

10 9 8 7 6 5 4 3 2 1
Printed in China
H13770320

Free Spirit Publishing Inc.
6325 Sandburg Road, Suite 100
Minneapolis, MN 55427-3674
(612) 338-2068
help4kids@freespirit.com
freespirit.com

FSC
www.fsc.org
MIX
Paper from
responsible sources
FSC® C144853

First published in Great Britain in 2020 by Wayland, an imprint of Hachette Children's Group

Text copyright © Hodder and Stoughton, 2020. Illustrations copyright © Hanane Kai, 2020. All rights reserved.

The rights of Hanane Kai to be identified as the illustrator of the Work have been asserted by her in accordance with the Copyright, Designs and Patents Act, 1988.

Edited by Sarah Peutrill. Designed by Hanane Kai. Texturing of illustrations by Mariela Gallegos.

Contents

There are things we all need to be able to live well and safely. These are called rights.

All people have equal value, and this means that all of us have equal rights. It doesn't matter if we are young or old, sick or healthy, poor or rich. It doesn't matter where we are born, what color our skin is, or what we believe.

There may be things you want, such as a trip to the zoo or a new toy. But these are different from the things you need. So how can we know the difference and decide what our rights are? How do we make sure that all the people in the world are treated equally and have what they need?

In 1948, a group of people from many countries agreed on a list of rights that all people have. This list is called the Universal Declaration of Human Rights. Since it was created a long time ago, we can keep adding to it, but it is a good place to start when we talk about human rights.

Universal Declaration of Human Rights

One of the most important of these human rights is the right to be alive and be safe. This is called the right to life.

Work is a very important part of life. People need to be able to work so that they have money to buy what they need— and even some things they want—and to take care of their families. Along with the right to work comes the right to rest, recover, and enjoy life.

Everyone has the right to be a free person and not be held in slavery. There are different kinds of slavery, but slaves are usually forced to work very hard for little or no pay.

All people deserve the chance to live a healthy life. They have the right to food, clothing, and a place to live. They should be able to see a doctor when they are sick. They should be able to get help if they lose their jobs or if they are too sick or elderly to care for themselves.

You might love going to school, or sometimes think you'd rather not go! But how would you feel if you couldn't ever go to school? All children have the right to go to school and get a good education, so they can succeed in life.

Everyone has the right to get married if they
want to and have children if they want them.
No one should be forced to get married if
they don't want to or if they are too young.

Everyone has the right to their own beliefs and opinions, as long as their beliefs do not cause them to harm others. People can be part of whatever religion they choose, or no religion, and they have the right to leave a religion if they want to. Diverse beliefs and opinions help people learn from each other and see other points of view.

Everyone deserves to be protected by just laws and have a fair trial in a court. A trial means that before anyone is put in prison, they can stand in front of a judge and sometimes a jury. The judge and jury listen to the story and look at evidence to decide if the person is innocent or guilty.

Even in prison, people have rights. All forms of torture go against human rights. Even if people have done something very bad, they should not be tortured.

If laws do not protect people in their own country, they have the right to leave. When people are in danger, they have the right to move to a new place and seek safety.

Unfortunately, sometimes countries do not want to welcome people who are trying to escape danger. Governments might ignore the human rights of these people and say that people from certain countries are not welcome.

Sadly, although we all have these human rights, the world is not fair and equal yet. Not everyone has the things they need, including safety, homes, and food.

People live in war zones, refugee camps, or places where there isn't enough food. Sometimes parents don't have enough money to send their children to school. Some countries have governments that are not fair. They may imprison or torture people who stand or speak out against them.

In places where not everyone has their rights respected, some people fight for equality. They are called human rights activists. Some activists may choose to protest. Others may choose to call or write to members of government to tell them when they see groups of people being treated poorly. Some become politicians themselves and try to fight for change.

21

Children have rights just as adults do. They have the right to food, a home, and care. They also have the right to play. Parents share responsibility for raising children and need to do what is best for them.

Governments should help parents care for their children by offering things like free schooling, healthcare, or money for housing when families need it.

Every single person can do things to make sure that those around them are treated with equality and respect.

Sometimes people bully others. They might make fun of someone for the way the person acts, speaks, dresses, or looks, or for no reason at all. Many times, the person bullying does not realize how hurtful their actions are. Defending someone who is being bullied, and asking the person *doing* the bullying to stop, is a brave way to fight for equality and inspire others to do the same.

It isn't always easy to stand up for human rights and equality, but it is the right thing to do. There will probably be times when you are not treated well, and you will want someone to stand up for you too.

Every day, people are working to make sure everyone's rights are protected. In what small or big ways can you fight for equality?

Find Out More

Books

Dreams of Freedom
Amnesty International, Lincoln Children's Books, 2015

Every Human Has Rights: A Photographic Declaration for Kids
National Geographic, 2008

I Have the Right to Be a Child
Alain Serres, Groundwood Books, 2012

Websites

Find out more about rights and equality and human rights activists: youthforhumanrights.org/what-are-human-rights

Save the Children is a charity that fights for children's rights: savethechildren.org

Watch a video describing young people's rights under international human rights law in friendly language: youtube.com/watch?v=COjVj9czgrY

Glossary

beliefs: ideas or values that people accept to be true

bullying: when someone repeatedly treats another person in a mean or unwanted way

equal: having the same value

government: the group of people who control and make decisions for a country

judge: an official who decides cases in a court

jury: a group of people who look at evidence in court to decide whether a person is innocent or guilty

opinions: views or ways of thinking that may not always be based on facts

politicians: people who are chosen to be part of a government

prison: a place where people are held when they have committed a crime or broken a law

refugee camps: temporary places where people stay when they are escaping war or hardship in their country

religion: a shared belief or system of beliefs that helps people find meaning in the world

responsibility: a duty to deal with something or take care of someone

rights: the things people need and should have to live well and safely

slavery: the practice of treating people as property and forcing them to work for little or no pay

torture: to cause deliberate harm to another person

More Great Books from Free Spirit

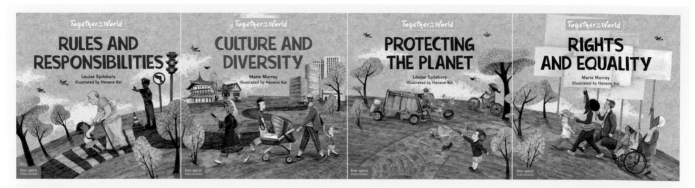

Together in Our World Series

The Together in Our World series addresses issues children are likely to hear about in the news and may not understand. In a straightforward and kid-friendly way, these picture books explain tough topics and offer readers ideas for what they can do to help make the world a better, fairer place.

Each book: 32 pp.; full-color; HC; 8½" x 8½"; ages 6–10

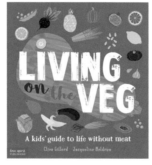

Go Green!
Join the green team and learn how to reduce, reuse, and recycle!
by Liz Gogerly, illustrated by Miguel Sanchez
48 pp.; HC; full-color; 8¼" x 10½"; ages 8–12.

Living on the Veg
A kids' guide to life without meat
by Clive Gifford and Jacqueline Meldrum
80 pp.; HC; full-color; 8¼" x 9"; ages 8–13.

Me and You and the Universe
written and illustrated by Bernardo Marçolla
36 pp.; HC w/ jacket; full-color;
8¼" x 9"; ages 3–8.

Interested in purchasing multiple quantities and receiving volume discounts?
Contact edsales@freespirit.com or call 1.800.735.7323 and ask for Education Sales.

Many Free Spirit authors are available for speaking engagements, workshops, and keynotes.
Contact speakers@freespirit.com or call 1.800.735.7323.

For pricing information, to place an order, or to request a free catalog, contact:

Free Spirit Publishing Inc. • 6325 Sandburg Road • Suite 100 • Minneapolis, MN 55427-3674
toll-free 800.735.7323 • local 612.338.2068 • fax 612.337.5050 • help4kids@freespirit.com • freespirit.com